W9-DFZ-494

PLANET
EARTH

ROCKS

Big
Buddy BOOKS
Planet Earth

ABDO
Publishing Company

Marcia Zappa

VISIT US AT
www.abdopublishing.com

Published by ABDO Publishing Company, 8000 West 78th Street, Edina, Minnesota 55439.

Copyright © 2011 by Abdo Consulting Group, Inc. International copyrights reserved in all countries. No part of this book may be reproduced in any form without written permission from the publisher. Big Buddy Books™ is a trademark and logo of ABDO Publishing Company.

Printed in the United States of America, North Mankato, Minnesota.
032010
092010

 PRINTED ON RECYCLED PAPER

Coordinating Series Editor: Rochelle Baltzer
Contributing Editors: Heidi M.D. Elston, Megan M. Gunderson, BreAnn Rumsch, Sarah Tieck
Graphic Design: Adam Craven
Cover Photograph: *Shutterstock*: Lindsay Douglas.
Interior Photographs/Illustrations: *iStockphoto*: ©iStockphoto.com/Terryfic3D (p. 27); NASA (p. 5); *Peter Arnold, Inc.*: Martial Aquarone (p. 13), STUART CHAPE (p. 9), S. J. Krasemann (p. 21), Matt Meadows (p. 23), J & L Weber (p. 25), WILDLIFE (p. 13); *Photo Researchers, Inc.*: Joel Arem (p. 23), Andrew J. Martinez (p. 17), Photo Researchers, Inc. (p. 4), Mark A. Schneider (pp. 11, 21), John Shaw (p. 19), Michael Szoenyi (p. 7), Dr. Keith Wheeler (p. 17), Charles D. Winters (p. 7); *Shutterstock*: Susan S. Carroll (p. 30), Jakub Cejpek (p. 12), Tatiana Grozetskaya (p. 5), Tom Grundy (p. 21), Christopher Halloran (p. 27), jan kranendonk (p. 5), Keith Levit (p. 21), Caitlin Mirra (p. 9), Mike Norton (p. 5), NY-P (p. 25), Elzbieta Sekowska (p. 15), SERGIO B. (p. 11), SNEHIT (p. 29).

Library of Congress Cataloging-in-Publication Data

Zappa, Marcia, 1985-
  Rocks / Marcia Zappa.
    p. cm. -- (Planet Earth)
  ISBN 978-1-61613-494-5
  1. Rocks--Juvenile literature. I. Title.
  QE432.2.Z37 2010
  552--dc22
                              2009053343

TABLE OF CONTENTS

THAT ROCKS!

Earth's surface contains many different substances. Some of these are water, soil, ice, and rocks. Underneath all this is rock!

Earth is largely made up of rock. Rock exists inside Earth, as well as on its surface. Rock is an important part of planet Earth.

SCIENCE SPOT

Earth has layers, like an onion. Earth's crust is made of loose rock and soil. Its mantle is solid rock. And, Earth's inner and outer cores are mostly made of the metals iron and nickel.

Crust

Mantle

Outer Core

Inner Core

Small rocks called pebbles line some beaches.

Giant rocks rise up to make mountain peaks.

Tiny rock pieces called sand fill deserts.

FROM THE INSIDE OUT

Rock is made of natural elements called minerals. Salt, gold, and graphite are all minerals.

Every mineral is made up of tiny parts called atoms. The atoms are in set amounts and patterns. This makes a mineral's insides the same all the way through.

Rock usually contains more than one type of mineral. So, its insides are varied.

SCIENCE SPOT

Many people use graphite every day. The lead in pencils is made of graphite!

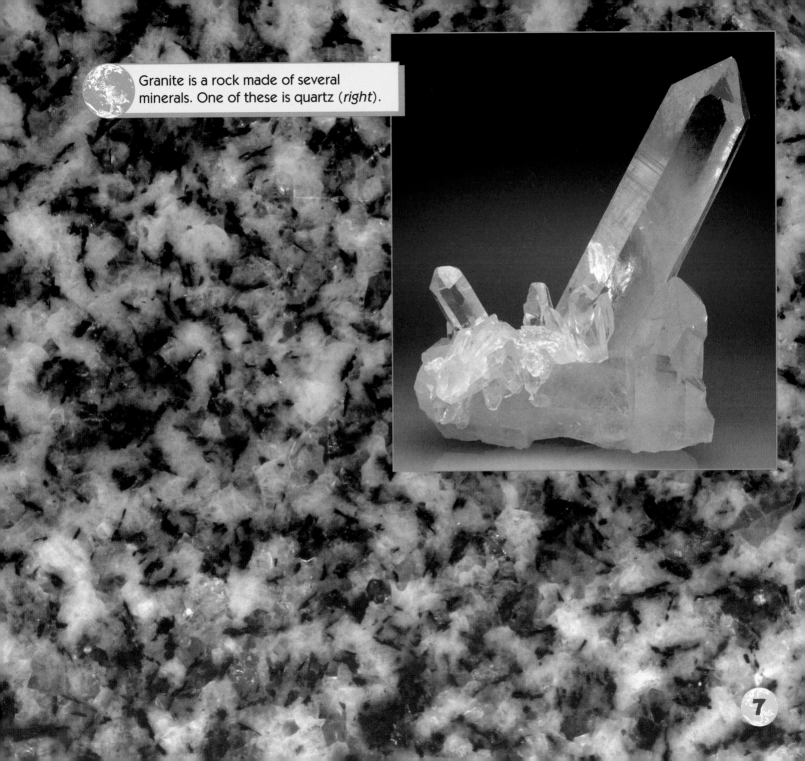

Granite is a rock made of several minerals. One of these is quartz (*right*).

Earth has many different types of rocks. Scientists sort them into three groups based on how they form. These groups are igneous (IHG-nee-uhs) rock, sedimentary (seh-duh-MEHN-tuh-ree) rock, and metamorphic (meh-tuh-MAWR-fihk) rock.

Rocks come in different shapes, sizes, and colors.

BURNING UP!

Igneous rocks are formed from hot, melted rock called magma. Magma is found deep inside Earth. When magma cools, it hardens into solid rock.

Some igneous rocks form when magma cools inside Earth. This can take thousands or even millions of years. These rocks tend to have large crystals.

When magma rises to Earth's surface it is called lava.

Pegmatite is an igneous rock formed inside Earth.

Sometimes, gas bubbles escape as magma quickly cools. This forms igneous rocks with holes in them. Pumice is one type of igneous rock. It can have so many holes that it floats on water!

Other igneous rocks form when magma cools above ground. Magma reaches Earth's surface in two ways. It can escape through deep cracks in the ground. Or, it can erupt from volcanoes.

Above ground, magma cools very quickly. So, igneous rocks form in just a few hours. These rocks don't have time to form many large crystals.

Obsidian is an igneous rock formed on Earth's surface.

PIECE BY PIECE

Sedimentary rocks form at or near Earth's surface. Most take thousands of years to form. They are built from sediments.

Sediments are small pieces of rock that have been worn away. This can be due to wind, water, or ice.

 Sedimentary rock is the most common type of rock near Earth's surface. It often has layers called strata.

SCIENCE SPOT

Sediments can also include the remains of plants and animals. When these remains harden, they become fossils. Scientists study fossils to learn about life on Earth millions of years ago.

Most sedimentary rocks form from pressure. Sediments pile up on land and in bodies of water. The weight of the pile creates pressure. This causes the bottom sediments to bond together. They harden into solid rock.

Other sedimentary rocks form from evaporation. Certain minerals dissolve in water. Later, the water evaporates, but these minerals remain. They bond together to form sedimentary rock.

SCIENCE SPOT

Salt forms when salt water evaporates.

Sedimentary rock covers most of the ocean floor. It also covers about 75 percent of Earth's land.

Shale is one common sedimentary rock.

17

CHANGING SHAPE

Metamorphic rocks form inside Earth. There, high heat and pressure change the structure of existing rocks. They create entirely new rocks!

Marble is a common metamorphic rock. It is formed from limestone.

THE ROCK CYCLE

All types of rock form from other rock. To explain this connection, scientists use the rock cycle. Rocks rarely move all the way through the cycle. They may stop, skip steps, repeat steps, and even go backward.

MAGMA

melts to form

cools to form

IGNEOUS ROCK

METAMORPHIC ROCK

gets buried, then heat and pressure are added to form

breaks down, then piles up to form

SEDIMENTARY ROCK

WHICH IS WHICH?

Scientists use several methods to identify rocks. To measure hardness, they scratch one rock against another. They rub a rock on a hard surface to find its streak color. And, scientists do experiments to learn what minerals make up a rock.

Hematite can be different colors. But, its streak is always dark red.

Quartz (*right*) is a hard rock. It can scratch softer rocks, such as calcite (*left*).

ENDLESS POSSIBILITIES

Rock has always been important to human life. Long ago, people used rocks for tools. Today, builders use granite and marble for floors and countertops. Special rocks, such as diamonds, are used for jewelry.

SCIENCE SPOT
Scientists called geologists study rocks. This tells them about Earth's history.

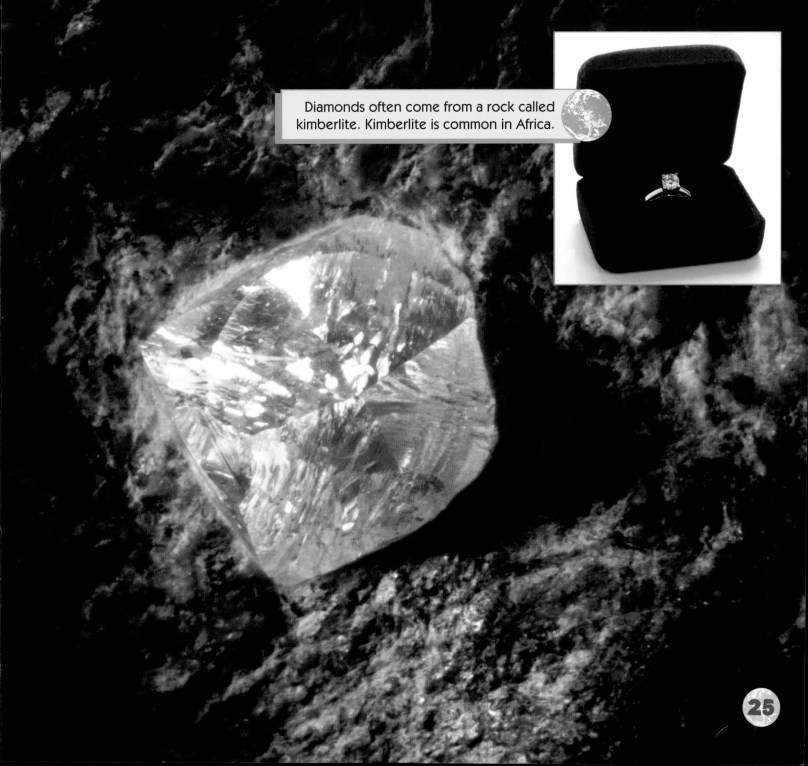

Diamonds often come from a rock called kimberlite. Kimberlite is common in Africa.

REMOVING ROCKS

In order for people to use rocks, they must gather them. Rocks inside Earth are gathered through a practice called mining.

Miners use powerful machines to remove rocks. Rocks deep inside Earth are gathered through underground mining. Rocks near Earth's surface are removed through surface mining.

Underground miners dig underground rooms and tunnels to reach rocks.

Surface miners remove the top layer of land to get the rocks below.

Mining rocks can harm Earth. Surface mining damages land. Plants may not grow on it.

People work to fix land after mining. This is called reclamation. Miners replace the top layer of land that had been removed. Then, they add trees and plants. This helps keep planet Earth healthy.

Rocks are an important part of Earth's natural wonder!

29

DOWN TO EARTH:
A FEW MORE FACTS ABOUT ROCKS

- There are about 3,000 known minerals on Earth.
- Soil contains tiny bits of rock. It also includes tiny plants and animals and their waste.
- Gemstones (*right*) are special minerals used for jewelry and decoration. They are usually see-through. And, they are cut and polished to sparkle.
- Many people collect rocks as a hobby. Rock collectors enjoy seeing how many different kinds they can find.

IMPORTANT WORDS

crystal (KRIHS-tuhl) a solid form made of atoms that have a repeating pattern.

dissolve (dih-ZAHLV) to become part of a liquid.

evaporate (ih-VA-puh-rayt) to change from liquid to vapor. The process of evaporating is called evaporation.

identify to find out what something is.

pressure (PREH-shuhr) the force applied to help move something.

structure (STRUHK-chuhr) the way something is put together.

varied having many types or arrangements.

volcano a mountain from which hot liquid rock or steam come out.

WEB SITES

To learn more about rocks, visit ABDO Publishing Company online. Web sites about rocks are featured on our Book Links page. These links are routinely monitored and updated to provide the most current information available.

www.abdopublishing.com

INDEX